# I CAN READ ABOUT

# MOTORCYCLES

Written by C. J. Naden

Illustrated by Herb Mott

**Troll Associates**

10  9  8  7  6  5  4  3  2

Many years ago, a German car maker hooked a gasoline engine onto a wooden bicycle frame. His funny-looking machine was the first real motorcycle or motorbike.

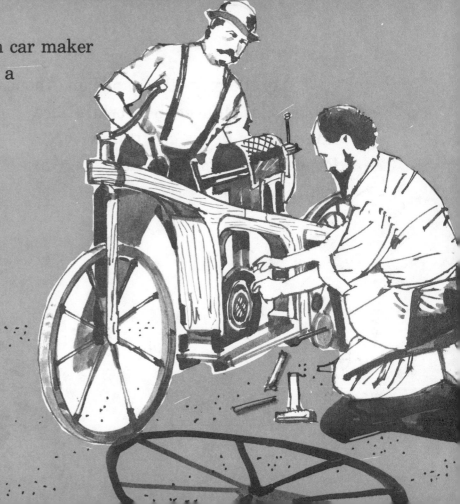

Today there are thousands and thousands of
motorcycles all over the world. Police
ride them in heavy city traffic.
People race them to see how
fast they can go.

All kinds of people ride them for
fun and transportation.

Riders often call
a motorcycle a *bike*. And
most motorcycles do look
like bicycles—except
for the engine and a
much heavier frame.

Many boys and girls
ride minibikes. A minibike
is the smallest of the cycles.
A minibike can be carried
in the back of a car.
It has a small engine
like the ones used on
power lawn mowers.

Minibike races are held every year.
Both boys and girls enter the races. Some of the
riders are young — less than ten years old.

A *minicycle* is another kind of
bike. It is a little larger,
a little faster, and a little
heavier than a minibike. It
has a small, motorcycle-type
engine. The minicycle looks
like a regular motorcycle,
only smaller.

Minibikes and minicycles are made for riding on trails and lanes.
They cannot be used on paved roads because they are so small.

*Z O O M* ...

Another cycle for off-road
riding is the *trail* bike.
It is much bigger and heavier
than the minibike or minicycle.
Trail bikes climb hills and zoom
over rough country at speeds
up to 70 miles, or 112 kilometers,
an hour.

Some motorcycles are made for riding on paved streets and roads.

*Touring bikes* are the giants of the motorcycle world.

They are heavy, and they can carry heavy loads. They can reach speeds of 100 miles, or 160 kilometers, an hour. They are popular for long distances, and cross-country travel.

The motorcycle you probably see most often is called a *street bike*. It is lighter than a touring bike. It can zoom around at 50 to 80 miles, or 80 to 128 kilometers, an hour. The street bike is a popular cycle for short trips and rides in town.

*Motor scooters* look different from most motorcycles. The scooter has a floorboard for the rider's feet. Other motorcycles have bars, called footrests, for the rider's feet.

The engine in a motor
scooter is over the rear
wheel, or in front of the
rear wheel. The engine
in other motorcycles
is halfway between
the two wheels.

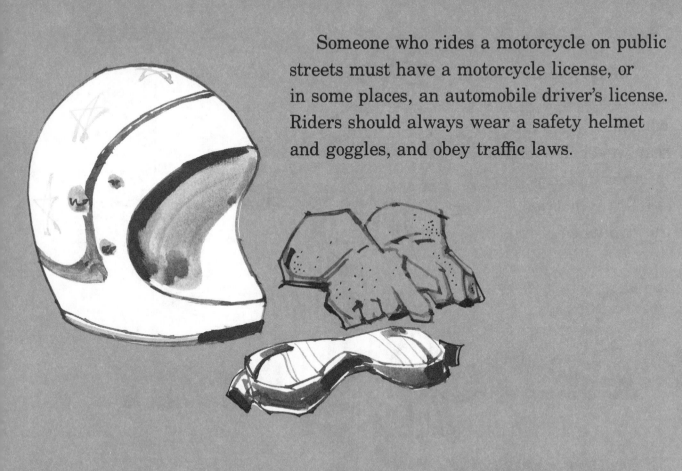

Someone who rides a motorcycle on public streets must have a motorcycle license, or in some places, an automobile driver's license. Riders should always wear a safety helmet and goggles, and obey traffic laws.

To ride on public roads, a bike must have
safety equipment — such as stoplights, good brakes,
headlights, a horn, and a rearview mirror.
Directional signals are important, too.

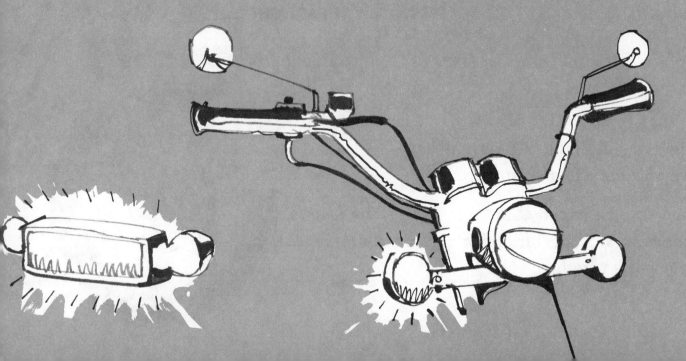

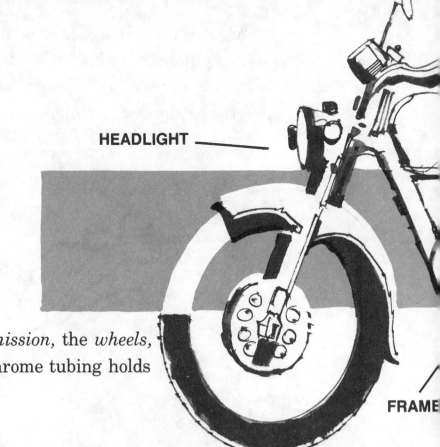

**HEADLIGHT** _____

Big or small, light or heavy, all motorcycles have four main parts.

They are the *engine*, the *transmission*, the *wheels,* and the *brakes*. A steel frame or chrome tubing holds the four parts together.

**FRAME**

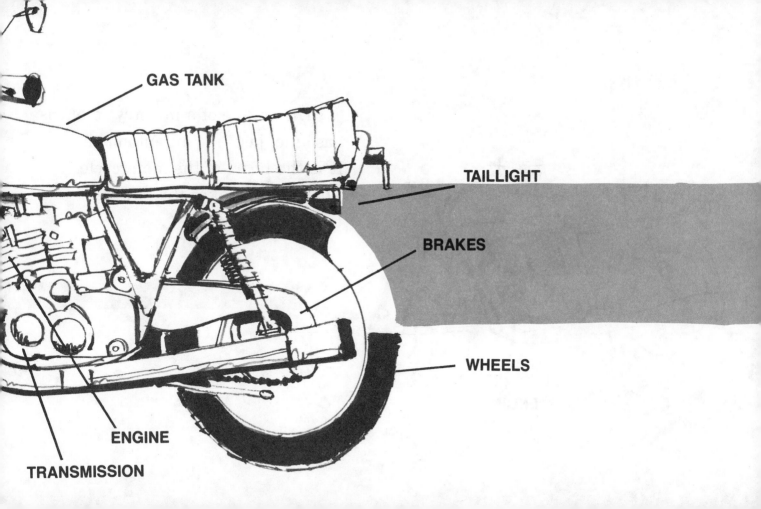

GAS TANK

TAILLIGHT

BRAKES

WHEELS

ENGINE

TRANSMISSION

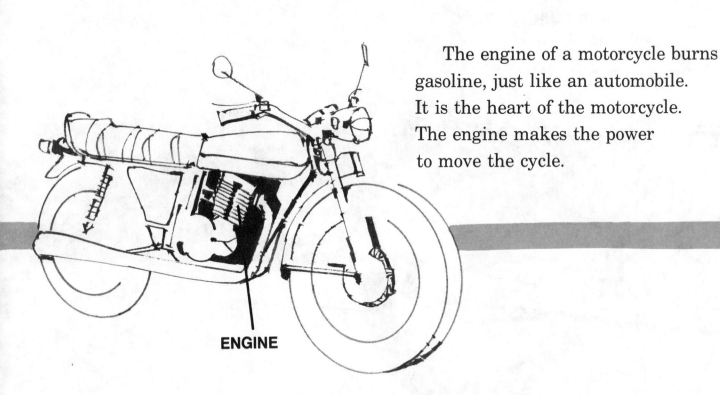

**ENGINE**

The engine of a motorcycle burns gasoline, just like an automobile. It is the heart of the motorcycle. The engine makes the power to move the cycle.

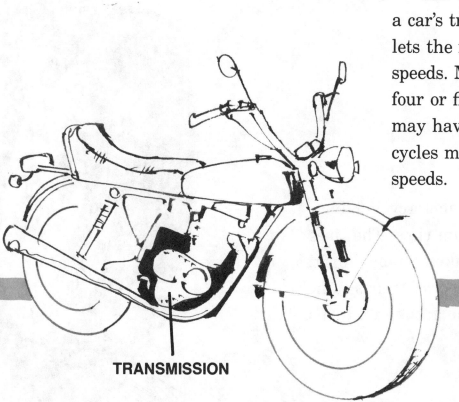

**TRANSMISSION**

The transmission works like a car's transmission. It lets the rider go at different speeds. Most motorcycles have four or five speeds. Small cycles may have three speeds. Racing cycles may have as many as eight speeds.

Wheels on a motorcycle have steel or aluminum rims. The tires are something like automobile tires. But they have special treads to help the cycle hug the ground on turns.

There are brakes on the front
and the rear wheels. Each brake
works by itself. But the front
brake can stop the motorcycle
faster and easier than the
rear brake.

Riding a motorcycle can be dangerous. There is very little to protect the rider from being thrown off the bike.
But if you obey safety rules, motorcycling can be a great deal of fun. It takes practice to ride a motorcycle well. But it isn't hard to learn how.

Most cycles have a lever that you must kick down to start the engine. Twisting your hand back and forth on the handle grip makes the engine run faster or slower. Most cycles have two hand levers. If you squeeze one hand lever, the engine will run, but the bike won't move. When you let go of the lever, the cycle goes forward. The other hand lever works the front brake. A foot pedal works the rear brake. Some cycles have a foot lever for shifting the gears in the transmission, while others have a hand lever.

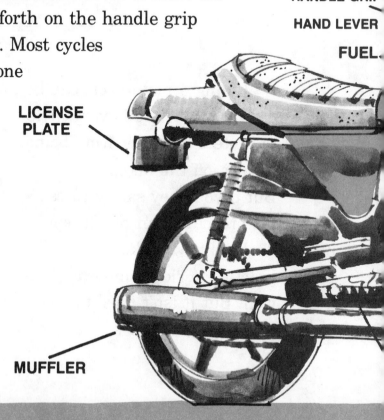

HANDLE GRIP

HAND LEVER

FUEL

LICENSE PLATE

MUFFLER

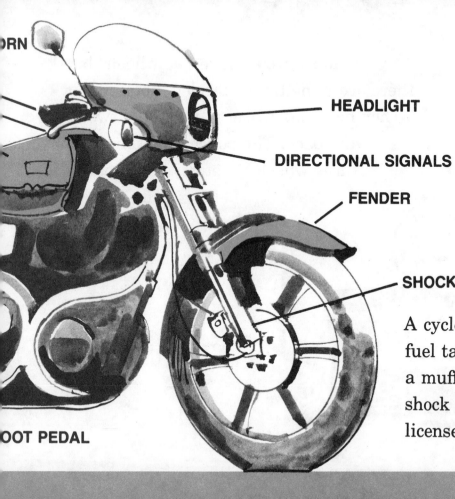

**HORN**

**HEADLIGHT**

**DIRECTIONAL SIGNALS**

**FENDER**

**SHOCK ABSORBERS**

**FOOT PEDAL**

A cycle has other parts too, such as a
fuel tank, a battery, fenders,
a muffler, a horn, lights,
shock absorbers, and
license plates.

Most cycles have two wheels, but there are some three-wheeled motorcycles. They have one wheel in front and two in the back. The police sometimes use three-wheeled motorcycles to patrol city streets.

Some cycles have sidecars attached to them. Someone hops into the sidecar and goes along for the ride.

Many people ride cycles just for fun.
Others ride to save on gasoline.
And some ride for the thrill
of motorcycle racing.

Professional motorcycle riders enter many different kinds of races. Each one wants to end the racing season as the best rider of all!

There are different kinds of motorcycles for different kinds of races. Fast road-racing machines are used in road-racing events. These cycles are built for speed.

Road racing is exciting, but it can be dangerous.
The rider leans forward and zooms around the track.
Riders can reach very fast speeds —
about 180 miles, or 288 kilometers,
an hour.

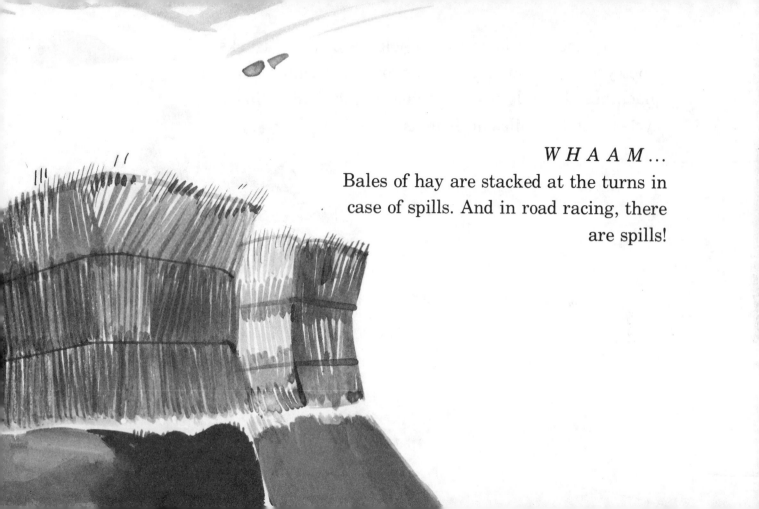

*WHAAM*...
Bales of hay are stacked at the turns in case of spills. And in road racing, there are spills!

Some motorcycle races are held on flat, dirt tracks.
The cycles used on these tracks are often called flat-track
machines. They do not go as fast as the road-racing
cycles, but 100 miles an hour is not slow!

Some cycle events are a real test for rider and cycle. In an enduro race, time is important. Each rider races against the clock. The course goes through woods and over hills. It goes across streams, and even through deep mud. You have to be rugged just to finish!

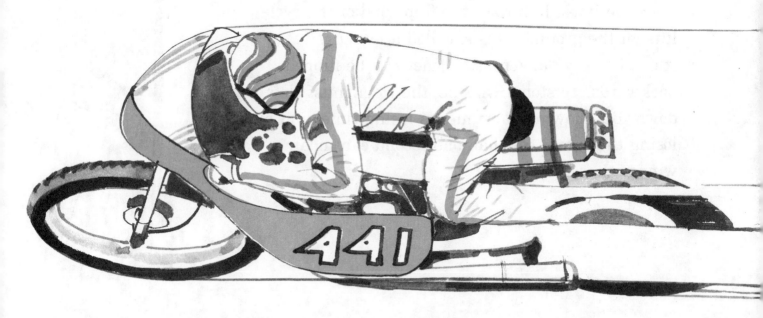

Drag racing cycles are used on short racing tracks.
Each race lasts only about 30 seconds!

Sometimes, in a race, the front end of the cycle lifts off the ground. This is called a *wheelie*. It can be very dangerous. A rider can be flipped backwards. To stop a wheelie, the rider must slow down. But slowing down means losing time, and maybe losing the race. Less than one second can mean a winner or a loser.

Each year, models of new
off-road motorcycles are shown
at the International Six-Days
Trial. Riders from many countries
enter this test of skill. The
Trial is held in a different
country each year.

There are many
different events during
the International Six-Days
Trial. There may be drag races,
cross-country contests, and hill-
climbs.

In a cross-country race, the noisy machines roar across dry, sandy deserts. This kind of racing is sometimes called "desert racing." The temperature can be very hot in summer and very cold in winter. It takes courage and a good cycle to win this kind of race.

Perhaps you'll be in a motorcycle race one day.
Remember what it takes to make a good cycle rider—
skill and practice, a bike in top condition,
and most of all...safety first!

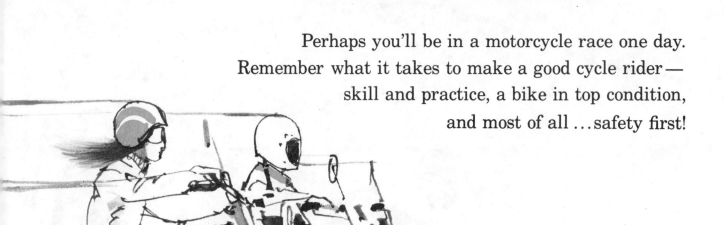